Before You Marry:

A Single's Guide to Choosing
and
Being God's Best Spouse

Jenifer Regennitter, MSEd, LCPC

Cover Art: **Val Muller**

DWB PUBLISHING
www.dancingwithbearpublishing.com

Contents

Foreword

According to the Center for Disease Control and Prevention, in 2009 provisional data showed that there were at least 140,509 marriages and at least 52,685 divorces. You've probably heard the arguments that no one understands commitment these days, or people give up too easily or they don't try hard enough to keep a marriage together. There are books by the hundreds, marriage retreats, seminars and groups to tell you how to have a successful marriage. However, succeeding in marriage begins with who we choose in the first place, and it is difficult to find many people in the church offering direction in that area.

As a group, singles are significantly under served in the church today, partly because most people do not realize that there are so many of us out there! The U.S. Census Bureau reported in 2010 that more than ¼ of the total population lived alone. That's more than 26 *million* people. Whether we have always been single or are single again, we as a group have the opportunity during this season of singleness to learn from others'—and our own—mistakes and be careful about choosing well for ourselves. In all areas of our life, we have the option to choose God's best for that situation, or less than His best. Now, it's not always black or white; not choosing God's best may not end in total disaster, but it will certainly never bring us the level of satisfaction and joy that His best brings. That's why we as singles need to so closely look at who we choose in relationships.

When the idea of writing this book began to bubble up in my spirit, I initially thought, "I can't do that. I've never been married. Who's going to listen to me?" I still don't know all the reasons God has kept me single this long, but He has certainly used this time to give me the opportunity to learn from others along the way by observing their marriages (good and not so good), either in my counseling career or in my personal life. I felt I needed to share with others what I've been blessed to learn so far.

I write this not as an expert in relationships, and certainly not from my own personal experience in marriage, but as a professional counselor and an observer of life. While this book does not and cannot cover all possible scenarios, potential issues or factors one must consider before choosing a spouse, it is designed to act as a springboard for deeper reflection, thought and discussion about the subject. My hope is that something in the pages of this book will help others make better choices, both in the type of person they choose, and the type of person they choose to be. Thank you to all my family and friends who have encouraged me and prayed for me along the way, and who I know will continue to do so.

Part One:
Choosing God's Best

~ One ~
Feeling Called

There's a cliché often offered to singles by people who are married, when asked, "How did you know this was *the one*?" The response is often a simple "I knew," to which many of us think, "Gee, thanks, that's so helpful..." Though people may not always be able to express what, "I knew," really means, I believe that statement deserves a deeper look. I cannot tell you how many couples I have talked to in which one or the other states there was a point in their relationship when God spoke into their spirit and said, *"This is who I have for you." Knowing*, as the world defines it, has more to do with making a logical, well thought out decision that makes sense on paper, or a vague sense of trusting what fate has put in your path and going with it, like trying to hit a bull's-eye in the dark and hoping it turns out okay.

In God's Kingdom, however, we are to be led by *His Voice*, and called by *His Spirit* in all the things we do. In John 10:27, Jesus says, *"My sheep listen to my voice; I know them and they follow me."* God also assures us in Jeremiah 29:11 that, *"I know the plans I have for you," declares the LORD, "plans to prosper you and not to harm you, plans to give you hope and a future."*

Though God is speaking to the people as a group in this passage, we can trust this also applies to us as individuals. Since God knows us, and knows the good plans He has for us, doesn't it make sense that He would also know the person He has created to be our spouse, and the good plans He has for them? Because God knows all the details about us—who would be best for us, and who we would be best for—it is that much more important that we do not rely on our own understanding (Proverbs 3:5), but seek God in who we choose.

So how can we "know" which person is the one He has created for us? Primarily, we can "know" by learning how to listen to and recognize the Holy Spirit's voice. I came into a personal relation-ship with Jesus at the age of eleven. Certainly, I can look back on my life and see His fingerprints all over it, but it was not until adulthood that I came to know the Holy Spirit as a separate but equally important part of God. In my church upbringing, the Holy Spirit was not discussed often. We all wore red on Pente-cost Sunday and read from the second chapter of Acts, but there was never any discussion about the important role the Spirit plays in our journey.

In John 14, Jesus talks about God sending the Holy Spirit as an advocate and spirit of truth to guide us until Jesus returns. The Holy Spirit is God's continuing presence with us. Learning to recognize the Spirit's leading was a significant turning point in my walk with God. Prior to this, life was sometimes like *Where's Waldo,* where you search long and hard for a tiny clue about what God wants you to do, and often end up taking a guess and hoping for the best. I would often ask God for a sign, and then wait for something magical to point me in the right direction.

Once I began to recognize how His Spirit speaks to me, leads, urges, and draws me, I learned to lock onto that feeling of peace and strength in my gut like tuning into a station on an old radio. I believe God purposely set it up this way, so we would have to be in an intimate relation-ship with Him to find direction. He wants to *lead* us through His relationship with us, and the time we spend with Him, not hand down a bunch of orders so we follow like a bunch of robots. The Lord *so* deeply desires intimacy with us. Making decisions in situations where the outcome is unknown is much easier when we have peace in our spirit that He is leading us there.

Certainly, God speaks to us through countless means, such as a song, a word from a friend, circumstances, or the

Bible. I've experienced many times in my life where things happen in such a way that it's clearly something God put together and cannot be considered coincidence. We should all remain open to how He wants to speak to us. But part of maturing in the Lord means learning what it feels like in our gut when the Spirit is urging us to do something, or speaking something into our hearts. If we cannot recognize His voice in other areas of our life, how can we recognize it when he brings our future spouse across our path? Hoping to find the right person without knowing how to hear and obey the Spirit is like setting out on a cross-country hike without a map or compass. You are likely to get lost, and possibly experience some negative, even harmful, consequences along the way.

     For anyone who has never experienced a relationship with the Holy Spirit, let me encourage you today, to ask God to give you His Spirit. Jesus tells us in Luke 11:13 that God will give His Spirit to those who ask. If you are persistent in asking for God's Spirit, I promise it will change your life for the better.

     One of the biggest revelations God has given me about marriage is that just as we are all called to an individual purpose in His Kingdom (Romans 8:28), couples are also called to a purpose in His Kingdom. The combination of a couples' personalities, strengths and gifts, allows God to show Himself through them in a unique way. Often, God will place people in a couples' path that need to see Him in the specific, unique way He shines through that couple. One couples' strengths may be exactly what others around them need to grow. However, the most important pur-pose for marriage is for God to use that marriage to impact His Kingdom. Just as His light shines uniquely through His children, it shines uniquely through married couples. The combination of a couples' personalities, strengths and gifts, allows God to show Himself in the specific way people He brings across that couple's path need to see Him. However, to know our purpose as a couple, we must first be able to hear the Holy Spirit, so we will know our individual purpose. When we know our individual purpose, we can better judge if a potential spouse is going to fit into that purpose. It is important that we ask ourselves, "Is this person going where I'm going? Are they on board with what God is doing in my life? Will they enhance what God is doing in my life, or distract me from my purpose?"

Maybe you feel you haven't fulfilled your purpose yet, but you have a sense of what it is supposed to be. Make sure the person you choose fits into that vision. Often, the couples I talk to have had the same vision on their heart for years, and part of how they knew they were called to be married was that shared vision. A shared vision of God's purpose is a key part of the glue that holds a marriage together.

Feeling called to a specific marriage is a vitally important point. Often, people seem to get married because they believe marriage is what is going to make them happy. However, *happiness is an emotion that comes and goes*. Unfortunately, when the relationship they thought would bring them happiness doesn't do that, they are disappointed and sometimes opt out of the marriage.

For years, I truly thought the reason I was generally unhappy in life was because I wasn't married. I built marriage up in my mind to be something that was going to fix my unhappiness, and until I had it I couldn't possibly enjoy life. Thankfully, God loved me enough to show me that is wrong thinking. If we are unhappy in our single life, we will be unhappy in married life. There are times in life that are routine and mundane. There are times that are challenging and stressful. All those things will continue to happen even when we're married, so if we haven't figured out how to maintain peace and joy in our circumstances as single persons, we won't be able to do it when we're married. (It is not our spouse's job to make sure we never have to feel anything uncomfortable, by the way. We are all responsible for our own feelings and how we manage them, even in the context of relationship.)

However, when we marry because we know we are called to be married to that specific person, that knowledge helps sustain us, and keep us in the relationship when we're going through hard times. Remember, all that we are, the reason we exist, is for *His* Kingdom and where it is going. The same applies to marriage.

Questions for Thought or Discussion

1. How do *you* recognize the Holy Spirit's voice? What areas of your life would you like to hear Him speak to you about? What could you do to develop your ability to discern His voice?

2. What are some of the reasons you desire to be married? Do some of your perceptions of marriage need to be more in line with what God wants for you?

3. Do you have a vision for your life, or a sense of what your purpose is in God's Kingdom? If so, what is it? How do you see a spouse fitting into that vision? How do your past relationships fit, or not fit, into that vision?

~ Two ~
Knowing a Tree by Its Fruit

One of the most important ways to recognize the Spirit's leading is to "recognize a tree by its fruit," (Luke 6:43—45). Paul tells us the fruit of the Spirit is love, joy, peace, patience, kindness, goodness, faithfulness, gentleness and self-control (Galatians 5:22). If we walk in the Spirit's ways, we should see this fruit in our lives. I often see well-meaning people, who have not been in a relationship with another Christian before, make the mistake of choosing someone because they go to church, or believe some of the same things, or, are willing to go to church with them. Unfortunately, those reasons by them-selves are not enough. Many people go to church every Sunday, are involved in Sunday school and committees, quote scripture, listen to Christian radio, and appear to have it all together spiritually. However, those behaviors are not true signs that a person has the Spirit of God in them.

As 1 Corinthians 13:1-3 explains, *"If I speak in the tongues of men or of angels, but do not have love, I am only a resounding gong or a clanging cymbal. If I have the gift of prophecy and can fathom all mysteries and all knowledge, and if I have a faith that can move mountains, but do not have love, I am nothing. If I give all I possess to the poor and give over my body to hardship that I may boast, but do not have love, I gain nothing,"*

Anyone can follow a set of religious rules of what to do or not do, but if someone has a true relationship with God, you will know it by the fruit shown in their lives. When we spend time with Him, it changes us to be more like Him. In other words, do you see this person walking in love, filled with joy and peace, exercising patience, kindness and goodness with others? Are they faithful in their work, commitments and friendships? Are they gentle in how they deal with others? Do they seem able to exercise a good amount of self-control? If the answer is no, that person may not be in a place with the Lord that will be healthy and life-giving for you. Relationships are meant to give life to each other, not deplete it. Below are some of the other types of "fruit" that should be present in the life of the person that is God's best for us.

Their gifts and talents will compliment yours. One thing I have observed about healthy, Godly marriages and relationships, is that peoples' gifts and talents tend to complement each other. Yes, they share the same values, similar interests, etc., but where one is weak the other is strong. Their gifts and strengths balance each other. If one is introverted, the other tends to be extroverted. Where one is organized and logical, the other is less organized, but more creative and "outside of the box" in their thinking. They are alike and different in ways that are important, but their differences always help each other grow. They do not hold each other back or bring each other down. Their differences, and similarities, enhance and strengthen the relationship, without either person having to change who they are fundamentally.

They love with God's heart. They have an ability to see the best in you, believe in you, rejoice over you, celebrate and encourage you. How do I know this? Because this is part of how God relates to us. He is enthusiastic about us, He believes in our ability to carry out His will (with and through Him), and He rejoices over us. He wants us to grow but doesn't condemn us for our weaknesses or shortcomings. This is part of why it is so important for us to choose someone who has a sincere relationship with God. If someone doesn't know God, how can they love you with God's heart?

1 Corinthians 13:4-7 describes what love is supposed

to be. *"Love is patient, love is kind. It does not envy, it does not boast, it is not proud. It does not dishonor others, it is not self-seeking, it is not easily angered, it keeps no record of wrongs. Love does not delight in evil but rejoices with the truth. It always protects, always trusts, always hopes, always perseveres."*

Note the key descriptive words here. Patience and kindness are, as we discussed, fruit of the Spirit. These descriptors of love reflect the fruit of patience and kindness, but also of gentleness, faithfulness, goodness and self-control. In other words, this is what God's heart for you and I looks like. This is love as God defines it, not as the world defines it. Movies and media focus on the romantic and physical part of love, which are things God created, and I believe He wants us to have. However, that part of love, by itself, is not enough to make an enjoyable marriage, let alone one that lasts. If someone truly knows Jesus, it will show in how they love others and you.

They have a desire to grow and to see you grow. God calls us all to grow more like Him every day. In Matthew 13, Jesus shares the parable of the seed sower. Much like the seed that hit hard ground and could not take root and grow, people sometimes are hard of heart and unwilling to grow. We cannot expect anyone to have all their issues straightened out before we consider them as a partner, but we can expect they be willing to examine their hearts and seek God on how He wants them to grow spiritually, relationally, professionally, and financially. This is important because, if we are trying to grow and our partner isn't, we will eventually begin to grow apart. It is inevitable.

We all start out in the shallow end of the pool spiritually and emotionally. At various points in life, though, God presents us with the chance to go deeper. If one is moving into the deep end of the pool but their spouse is content to stay in the shallow end, they will inevitably grow apart. For relationships to be strong and stay strong, people must go in the same direction, and have the same vision for their marriage. This may seem obvious, but in truth, there are many marriages that involve two people leading almost completely separate lives. They don't spend time together, they don't communicate, they don't pray together, and therefore have problems making decisions together because they simply aren't on the same page. Sadly, some end up living like roommates, being married on paper but alone in every other way. Having a vision for our purpose and direction in life, both individually and as a couple, helps us stay focused and on course. Being able to move forward on that course requires us to grow and mature. So naturally, it follows that God's best for us is someone who also wants to grow, and not stay stagnate.

In the same way, God's best for us is *not* someone who will draw us away from God, but will help us grow closer to Him. For example, if someone is pressuring their intended to do things that are clearly against God's Word, watch out! If they're pressuring that person to have sex outside of marriage, do drugs, steal, lie, or do anything that goes against God's will, that is *not* someone who supports spiritual growth, but is actually trying to move that person away from God.

In fact, God's best should lovingly holding us accountable in our spiritual life, and challenge us in areas where we may need to step it up. God's best will not be someone who resents your time in Bible study, prayer, or involvement in church (assuming you are keeping it in balance). I have heard had people say that one of the most attractive things to a Godly man is a Godly woman. I've heard wives talk about how precious it is to wake up in the morning and see their husbands reading scripture and praying. God's best will celebrate your spiritual growth, not resent it. Your intended should be excited about what God is doing in your life, where He is taking you, and wants to be an active part of it. In too many marriages, it seems as if one person does all the spiritual work, while the other is off doing their own thing, or worse yet, tries to interfere with their spouse's growth.

It's important that we understand, however, that God wants us to be ministering and growing *together*.

Let's look at Susan's story. Susan is a divorced mother of two who recently jumped back into the dating scene. She loves teaching a children's Sunday school class at her church, and volunteers much of her extra time serving there. She has always had a passion for children and feels called to teach them, not only math and reading, but also about Jesus. She gets great joy out of seeing little hands folded in prayer, or asking Jesus into their hearts, and it fills her with a great sense of purpose.

The years since her divorce have been primarily focused on caring for her kids, but she is lonely and longing for some companionship and romance. Around this time she met Rob through a dating website. They decided to meet over coffee and the attraction was instant. They agree to see each other again, and Susan is thrilled. Here is an attractive, charismatic man who is actually interested in *her*. Rob is nothing like her ex-husband. He is exciting, funny, and his smile makes her melt. *Surely this wouldn't be happening if it wasn't from God.* She smiles at the thought.

The relationship grows and they spend more and more time together. Although Susan is disappointed her new friend will not attend church with her, she decides all relationships require compromise and shrugs it off. After dating for nine months, they become engaged and eventually marry. This marriage is going to last, she is sure of it.

About a year into the marriage, however, Rob begins to complain about her volunteering at the church. He insists she is spending too much time there, and he feels neglected. The issue sparks some arguments between them and Susan starts to feel a distance in their relationship. Determined not to go through another divorce, she tells herself that as much as she loves her church family, she must do whatever it takes to make this marriage work.

As time goes on, however, her friends at church begin to express some concern that she hasn't been around. Even her sister asks if everything is alright since she's noticed Susan seems to be unhappy when she typically is a joyful person. Eventually, Susan begins to realize that though Rob no longer complains about how she spends her time, she is struggling with a growing emptiness and sense of monotony in her day-to-day existence. She is spiritually dehydrated and realizes that without the connection of her church family, her relationship with God has become stale and stagnant.

When she attempts to talk with Rob about it, he is only resentful. Why does she need to waste her time with this "church stuff" when she should be at home spending time with him? Isn't he enough? At this point Susan is faced with an agonizing tug of war. How can she invest in her relationship with God if it threatens to end her marriage? How can she save her marriage if the cost is her relationship with God?

From Susan and Rob's story, we can see that although they shared a mutual attraction, they did not share a common vision or goals. Susan's Sunday school class was her ministry but in her effort to compromise, she actually settled. She chose someone who did not share a passion for her ministry, and therefore, did not support her, and in the end he pulled her away from her calling. When we are not fulfilling our calling, we are not fulfilled as people.

Rob could not help Susan grow spiritually because he was spiritually dead himself. Remember, church, support groups, Bible study, and anything else that helps us grow spiritually is not a habit or hobby. These events are a vital part of our spiritual and emotional health. Feel free to compromise on interests such as sports, music, hunting, or movies, but keep straight the things in life that are non-negotiable, and must remain in place in order to be healthy.

Another place Susan could have chosen differently is in thinking more specifically about her vision for her life. She knew she loved serving at her church, but perhaps she didn't take time to think about what specific character-istics she needed in a mate to compliment that vision. Like throwing a dart while blindfolded, if we don't identify those characteristics we need in another, we are likely to miss the mark when it comes time to choose.

Susan also mistakenly thought because this attract-tive man was interested in her, that this *must* be from God. She chose to ignore the signs, or fruit that were in front of her that were clear indicators this was *not* from God. God is never going to send us someone who does not have a relationship with Him, or who would interfere with our relationship with Him. Our relationship with Him is His top priority and it's important that it remain ours. We must love Him first and most!

Questions for Thought or Discussion

1. Think about some of your last relationship. Did that person's life have evidence of the fruits of the Spirit? If so, how? If not, what red flags were present at the time that might have been an indication that person was not God's best for you?

2. Have you known someone in your life that showed you the type of love described in 1 Corinthians? How does it feel when someone loves you that way? How did it affect you as a person? What could you learn from that experience that might help you choose better in future romantic relationships?

3. Have you been in a relationship (friendship, co-worker, romantic, etc.) with someone that appeared to hold all the right Christian values but lacked maturity or depth in their walk? What were some of the challenges you found in that relationship as they relate to this specific issue?

4. What other fruit do you think it is important to look for that reflects God's best for us?

5. What do you think has helped lead you to choose God's best in other areas of your life? What has caused you to settle for less than His best? How might you apply those experiences to help you choose a spouse?

~ Three ~
Red Flags

So far we've talked about types of things to look for in a potential spouse. Now, let's talk about what to watch *out* for. Anyone I've talked to that has gone through divorce can tell me things they can identify, looking back, that should have been warning signs that something wasn't right. They say hindsight is 20/20, but as singles, we have the opportunity to learn from such mistakes. If you are in a relationship and having doubts, don't sweep them under a rug, minimize, or ignore them. As uncomfortable as it can be at times to acknowledge that a relationship may not be working out, it is much less painful to end it before marriage, than be forced to acknowledge it via divorce (and less expensive, I might add). Some common red flags to watch out for include:

Fighting and arguing. Of course, most couples have disagreements and some can be more heated than others, but most of your time together should not be involved in fights. Again, two fruits of the Spirit are peace and joy, which are opposite of constant arguing. Look closely at a potential spouse. Do they tend to want to draw you into a debate much of the time? Do they constantly correct what you say and insist they are right about everything? Do they listen to your opinion and feelings, or do they minimize them? Do they hold every mistake you've made against you to use during disagreements? Someone with God's heart for you will not want to tear you down, but build you up. When disagreements do happen, they are willing to handle them in a way that brings about solutions, not hurt feelings, because your relationship is more import-ant to them than winning an argument.

Cheating. As we talked about earlier, another fruit of the Spirit is faithfulness. I am always surprised by the number of people who will marry someone who cheated on them while they were dating, and then be hurt and surprised when that person continues to cheat during the marriage. Being married doesn't make a person faithful. Faithfulness is a character issue. God will never desire for us to be dishonored by someone who cheats and breaks our trust. Now yes, sometimes people can be genuinely remorseful and make the choice to grow and change. If they aren't, then we can be confident they are not God's best for us at this time.

Abusive behavior. Do not be confused. If someone is keeping track of your every move, telling you what to wear, what to say, who you can be friends with, who you can talk to, etc. they are *not* God's best for you. If they tear you down, insult you, or constantly criticize you, they are *not* God's best for you. Certainly, if they are physically harming you, they are *not* God's best for you. If you are not allowed to have opinions, needs or feelings of your own, that is abuse. If that person manipulates you into feeling guilty for having even a tiny bit of independence, that is also abusive. God *will never* desire for us to be abused— period. Some people grow up in abusive situations that were beyond their control, but as adults, we can make a choice and get out. Let me encourage you, (and I'm talking to women *and* men here), if you think you are in an abusive situation, *get help.* Do not think that the situation will get better once you are married. It is likely to only get worse. Talking to a counselor, support group, pastor, friend or even the police if need be, is a great way to make that first step toward something much better. Remember, God's best for us brings out our strengths and helps us grow. They will bring joy, peace and gentleness to the relationship, not fear, hurt and anger.

No walk with God. Again, this may seem obvious, but I see so many people who love Jesus marry someone who doesn't identify themselves as Christians at all. They say things like, "well, he's not a Christian now, but he may become one," or "at least she's willing to go to church with me, that's good enough." It is never a good idea to enter a relationship with the belief that you can change that person. That never works well, especially where our spiritual walk is concerned.

Susan and Rob's story illustrated this in chapter two. If you know the Lord, regardless of how long you've known Him, do not settle for someone who is not in the same place you are spiritually, or who is not going the same direction as you. Don't choose someone who is "backsliding," or losing ground, in their walk with God and expect to save them. That's not your job. They are responsible for their own spiritual walk, just as you are responsible for yours.

By the same token, don't settle for someone who is spiritually stagnant and not growing. Just because they are willing to attend church with you, or allow you go to Bible study, prayer group, etc. does not mean they are on the same spiritual level as you. Remember, we are called to marriage with a specific person because of how God wants to work through us *both* in the Kingdom. In order for Him to use us, we must *both* have a relationship with Him. It's that simple.

Consider the following scenario. Justin is a young, single guy who has been dating various girls on and off for several years, but has never gotten serious about anyone. He feels he is getting to the age where he needs to settle down and begins to feel a sense of urgency about doing so. He had his career and home established, and all he felt that was missing was a good wife. About this time, his coworker sets him up with a friend, Sonya, saying she and Justin may hit it off. Justin finds Sonya to be absolutely wonderful. She's gorgeous, a good cook, and she seems like the kind of woman that would fit into his life.

The two become serious quickly. Justin proposes after four months of dating, feeling eager to begin his new life. Sonya, however, is not ready for that, and suggests they live together as a trial run. Though it goes against his upbringing, he agrees, and they move in together. Justin thinks that after a few months, Sonya will see how wonderful they are together, and want to get married then, so no big deal.

His buddies are not as impressed with Sonya, and question Justin about some of her behavior, but Justin is willing to overlook things if it means not being alone. Big deal, so he'd caught her in a couple little white lies—didn't everyone do that from time to time? So what if sometimes she lost her temper and called him names? She only got upset because she was hormonal at the time and she never means what she says when she's like that. Hey, no one's perfect, right? Three years later, though, they are still not married, (because Sonya is still "not ready" yet), and living together with their son.

What started as white lies became overt lies about how and where she spent her money and time. Her temper tantrums had become more frequent and unpredictable, and there was almost constant conflict between them. As much as Justin would like to get out of the relationship, he feels obligated to stay because of his son. Even if his son wasn't involved, he couldn't afford to financially leave. So he is stuck, frustrated and confused. How did he get himself into this mess? Where did things go wrong? How did he not see this coming?

In Justin's case, his fear of being alone, and impatience about settling down, caused him to ignore several red flags that were in place early on in the relation-ship. Red flags aren't always like a giant billboard in the beginning. Sometimes, they start small and seem almost unimportant. But little red flags can grow into giant red banners if ignored. It's important we don't minimize negative behaviors and unhealthy aspects in our relationships. Those things *are* a big deal, and if we confront them now, we can potentially avoid some heartbreaking and complicated situations down the road. Many of us know someone who died of cancer that was detected only after it had spread too far to be treatable, and if the person had gone to the doctor when the symptoms started, they might have been spared. Relationships are the same way.

Red flags are warning signs of an unhealthy relationship. They are there if we know what to look for, and choose to acknowledge instead of avoid them. When we have clear standards in our mind of what is, and is not, acceptable, we are less likely to settle for inappropriate behavior from another person. As hard as it can be to be single, it is not worse than being in an unhealthy relationship.

Questions for Thought or Discussion

1. What red flags did you see in Justin's story that he ignored?

2. Looking back on some of your past relationships, what red flags were present that perhaps you did not notice or pay attention to at the time? Would recognizing them at the time have caused you to choose differently in that relationship and if so, how?

3. What are some other red flags you think it is important to watch out for? Why specifically do you think they are signs of an unhealthy relationship?

4. As a Christian, have you been in a relationship with a non-Christian before (or vice-versa)? How did the difference in your beliefs affect your relationship with that person and with God?

5. Have you been in an abusive relationship before? How did you get out? What did you learn from that experience that could help you choose better in the future?

~ *Four* ~
Check Yourself

$\mathcal{O}$ur ability to choose wisely also involves being aware of our motivation for choosing certain people. Many people who've been through the break-up of a relationship will say, "You know, looking back, I never should have gone out with them in the first place. I think the reason I was attracted to them was *(fill in the blank)*, not because of who they were." We sometimes realize, looking back, that there were other issues influencing our decision to choose that person. Sometimes, however, people fall into a pattern but have no insight as to why they always end up in unhealthy relationships.

Why do I always end up with men that cheat on me? Why is every woman I date so controlling? Why can't I find someone who isn't abusive? It's important that we be keenly aware of what attracts us to certain types of people, and to take an honest look at why those attributes attract us. Some attributes we find attractive might be healthy and others may be toxic. In this chapter, let's look at some common issues that may lead us into such potentially toxic relationships.

An important question to ask ourselves is, "What specifically do I like about being with this person?" Ever meet one of those people who seem to have some kind of supermodel on their arm? A Heidi Klum look-alike, or some guy who looks like he came from the pages of GQ? We see this in Hollywood all the time—beautiful couples who look great together and seem to be perfectly matched. Too often, though, the relationship ends, and they're both on to new relationships with other beautiful people, till those relationships end, and so on. Now, beautiful people can also be beautiful on the inside, but one of the major mistakes people seem to make is choosing someone based primarily on how they look, (and often not being honest about that).

1 Samuel 16:7 tells us that, *"people look at the outward appearance, but the LORD looks at the heart."* In this story, God chose David to be ruler rather than Eliab, or David's older brothers, (who were much bigger in stature), because of the condition of David's heart. Others may have looked more like what people expected a ruler to look like but David had the heart to be the kind of ruler they *needed*.

God couldn't have shown us any more clearly how much more important a person's heart is than their appearance than in His Son, Jesus. We know from scripture that Jesus wasn't necessarily all that much to look at. There was nothing about Him physically that was particularly attractive. Yet, no one has ever had, before or since, such limitless love, such boundless compassion for people. How much more clearly can God say to us that what is most important is a person's heart and character, not their physical appearance?

Yes, physical attraction is an important part of any marriage, after all, God created it. But when we choose primarily because we find someone physically attractive, we miss out on a relationship of depth. Building a relationship on physical attraction is like building a house on sand. When your looks start to fade as you age, the everyday routine sets in and the "spark" isn't there, you have no solid foundation to stand on. A strong marriage is built on a deep spiritual and emotional attraction, and an abiding friendship. *That* is what makes marriage last.

When you enjoy sharing mundane, everyday experiences with someone and can share your most intimate feelings because of the deep emotional and spiritual connection you share, then you have a strong foundation that can stand the trials of life. We need to watch for this type of connection in our dating life to help us choose the right person.

Another common issue is when people are attracted to people who need them. We all need others, and we all like to feel needed. Some people, though, are not happy unless they have someone who desperately needs to be rescued, fixed or saved. This way of relating to others is known as codependency, and it involves either weak or non-existent boundaries. It's important to know where I end and you begin. This includes knowing what things I can help you with, and what things are your responsibility to figure out. We'll talk more about boundaries in part two of this book. For now, though, it's important to be aware if this is an issue for you. Do you enjoy being with that person because they usually have some kind of drama, or problem, they can't fix without your help? How often do they attend to your needs and feelings? Do you feel like you're losing your own identity? In other words, who are you apart from that person? If you can't answer that question, that's a major red flag that this relationship has a lack of boundaries.

Another potential issue involves a fear of being alone. Are you with this person because you enjoy who they are and who you are around them, or, are you attracted to the idea of having someone there so you don't have to be alone? Does the idea of being on your own for any extended period of time increase your anxiety? If so, let me encourage you to take a serious look at why you are so afraid of being alone. Yes, we know God is always with us and has promised never to leave us, but let's be honest, no matter how much we love God, we still need people. A popular lyric I hear in some Christian music is, "You are all I need." However, I'm not convinced this is true for us, and I believe rather than be angry with us for that, God understands it. For example, when God created Adam and realized Adam needed a spouse, He didn't respond with anger

and say to him, "I am all you need. I should be enough."
Instead, he responded to Adam's need for companionship
by creating companions for him. He created all the animals
and birds, and most importantly, Eve.

I once had a well-meaning pastor say to me, "I've
never been lonely since I met Jesus." Of course, he also
met his wife when they were eighteen and married at the
age of twenty, so he'd never had to be alone as an adult.
Given his history, it makes sense he'd never been lonely.
Feeling lonely is *not* a sin. We are created to need people
in addition to God. In Matthew 22:37-39, Jesus gives us
what is known as *The Great Commandment*."

*"Love the Lord your God with all your heart and
with all your soul and with all your mind. This is the first
and greatest commandment. And the second is like it: Love
your neighbor as yourself."*

Loving God, and loving each other, is what we were
created to do, so it is natural to long for connection and
companionship with another.

Loneliness becomes a problem when we allow it to
torment us and cause us to choose less than God's best just
to have someone around. For many years, I struggled with a
persistent, tormenting level of loneliness. Even though I
loved my friends, I was often lonely and I couldn't seem to
shake it. It kept me from experiencing much joy in life, and
I went through many years just going through the motions,
simply existing. I truly believed that because I was single,
that must be the sole cause of my unhappiness, and if I
could be married, that would fix it! I would never have to
be lonely again.

Thank God He showed me that the real problem was
my tendency to be too private and keep others at a certain
distance. I had to learn to let people in, to go deeper in
my relationship with the Lord to fill that empty hole in my
heart. Had I not gotten this lesson, I can assure you, I
would have settled, ended up in a dissatisfying marriage,

and still found myself dealing with the same tormenting unhappiness. We need to be able to be comfortable being alone with ourselves. Even when we're married, our spouse cannot be with us every single minute. A human being cannot be our everything, or the only thing that brings us joy in life. If they are, that's another sign of codependency or at the least, poor boundaries on our part.

It's a dangerous position to put ourselves in. If that person dies, leaves, or is stricken with a serious illness that leaves them unable to care for themselves, we lose our only source of joy in life, and are left struggling to pick up the pieces.

Psalm 145:16 says *"You satisfy the desire of every living thing"*.

While God certainly does this, in part, by putting relationships in our life, our joy must come from the Lord first, then people. While friends and family can bring incredible joy, no one but God can make us feel truly satisfied in life.

One final common issue I sometimes see is when people choose someone because they are either just like, or just the opposite of, someone else. Their dad was an alcoholic, so they end up choosing men who are also alcoholics. Maybe they grew up feeling ignored or neglected, so they choose partners that are controlling because initially, it feels good to be the center of someone's attention. Their ex-wife was boring, so their new wife is the opposite, adventurous and full of drama. Maybe their last relationship was abusive, so they end up choosing someone who may not be abusive, but is still unhealthy in other ways (but convince themselves this person is great because "at least they don't abuse me.")

The point is, we all have baggage and issues. It's just part of living in this world. Having baggage isn't the problem. Not dealing with the baggage becomes the problem. When we don't look at ourselves, figure out what our issues are, and seek help to work through those issues, it is certain to negatively influence the way we go about choosing a spouse.

What specifically does "working through our issues" mean? It means knowing our insecurities, our weaknesses, our hurts that haven't healed, our wounded places, our fears, and our misguided beliefs about ourselves and others. It means getting rid of beliefs that are incorrect or unhealthy and replacing them with God's truth about us and others. It means asking God to come in and heal us where we're hurt, so we can be free to move forward. It means asking God to show us how He looks at us, and what He thinks about us, so that we can begin to see ourselves through His eyes and get rid of old insecurities that hold us back.

There's a saying in my business. "You can deal with it now or deal with it later, but eventually you're *going* to deal with it." Dealing with it later usually means many consequences, broken relationships, and stressful situations that (I promise you), are all a lot more uncomfortable to go through than looking at our issues now. It can be painful and scary to look at those things and let God into those areas, but the outcome will always be a healthier, happier, more peaceful version of our selves. We cannot hope to choose God's best for us when our judgment is clouded by unresolved personal issues. If you have not made this step, I encourage you to seek out a Christian counselor and/or support group that can help you begin the process.

Questions for Thought and Discussion

1. What has attracted you to certain people in the past? What attracts you now? Has what you find attractive changed over time and if so, how?

2. To what degree do you experience loneliness in your life? How do you deal with your loneliness? How might you deal with it differently in the future?

3. How comfortable are you with the thought of being alone? How has fear of being alone influenced who you've chosen in relationships?

4. Do you experience true joy in God? To what degree do you feel satisfied in Him?

5. How would you describe your level of trust in God to bring you a spouse? How do you deal with moments of doubt? What specifically do you think you need to address to help you trust Him more?

Part Two:
Being God's Best

~ Five ~
It Takes Two

In part one, we talked about factors that are important in choosing God's best. However, relationships take both people working at it to make it a success. So now we're going to talk about what we need to do to be God's best for someone else. I want to emphasize that just as in part one, we talked about our spouse not being perfect, but neither can we expect to be perfect ourselves. Being God's best doesn't mean we are without flaws. Being God's best means we are open to His leading, seeking His heart, and allowing Him to mold us into more usable vessels. Many of us have spent a lot of time thinking and praying about what we want in a spouse, but have you ever asked your-self if you are what someone else is praying for? Can we honestly say we are the best version of ourselves that we know how to be at the moment? Are we in a position to be a blessing to someone else?

We need to be careful about focusing so much on what we want from someone else that we neglect to take inventory of our own life and examine our own hearts. Remember, marriage doesn't exist just so we can be happy. Marriage exists so that God can use us as a couple and work through our marriage to make a difference in his Kingdom. For us to be poised to be used in that way, we have to be open to growing the way God wants us to grow. Marriage isn't all about "me". In fact, *life* isn't all about "me". Life and marriage are about the needs of His King-dom. Being unwilling to take ownership of our part in a relationship is selfish. If we are not willing to acknowledge the areas we need to work on now, it is not likely we'll be willing to do that in a relationship where there is a much more intimate, personal level of accountability (or should be). Why should God bring us His best if we cannot be His best for someone else?

Think of it like this. In most college classes, on the first day the professor gives you a syllabus that outlines when projects are due and tests will be given throughout the course. For illustration's sake, let's say this is the professor's promise to you that these things are going to happen and they will count for X percent of your overall grade, so you know up front which tests, or projects, are the most important.

Now, some of us in college were hyper-vigilant about this sort of thing and studied hard so that by the time final exams came, we felt prepared. Some of us chose to focus on living the college life and enjoying our friends, figuring we could just pull an all-nighter before the final exam and pass with no problem. Most of the time, which type of student would you expect to do well on the final? Which type of student would you expect to retain the information after the class is over so they can apply it to their career? Obviously, the better prepared student is typically going to do much better on both counts.

The same is true in relationships. If you have the desire in your heart to be married, and to share a life with someone, then consider that God's promise to you. You are called to that type of relationship and it will happen some-day. While you may not know the exact day it will happen, you will be much better prepared for that relationship if you recognize what it will take to make it thrive, and start working on those things now.

Identifying potential pitfalls, or areas of weakness, and strengthening them now will only help you do better when the time for marriage arrives. Preparing ourselves for marriage requires us to invest in that marriage before it happens. Every time we choose to acknowledge a fault, set a goal, raise our standards, go deeper in our relationship with God, and improve how we behave in relationships with people, we are investing in our marriage. We are preparing the soil in which our marriage will be planted, making sure it has the nutrients it needs to be healthy, and we have the skills to make sure it thrives. The better the soil, the deeper our roots, and the roots of that relationship will grow. The deeper the roots, the stronger we will be to stand up to the storms of life that will inevitably blow our way. It is the law of reaping and sowing. If we sow selfishness, bitterness, anger, deceit, fear and jealousy now, we will reap those things in our marriage. They will follow us there. If we sow humility, forgiveness, love, patience, tenderness and honesty now, we will reap the harvest of a marriage that is a blessing to us and those whose lives we touch.

Let's also consider that for some, the marriage God has called us to may involve children. Perhaps you have children of your own from previous relationships. Perhaps you plan to have children one day, or perhaps God will call you to be an incredible step-parent to a child who needs one. For us to have a positive influence on the children God places in our lives, we must be at our best. If God is calling you to be an example to a child, that child needs us to live in such a way that we can be a living example of God's love, so they can develop their own relationship with Him, and fulfill their own purpose in the Kingdom.

Too often, we don't realize how the choices we make in relationships affect the children involved. The way we live in our marriage will be the most influential example of a relationship they will experience in childhood. Whether it's your first marriage or not, any opportunity children have to witness what a loving, healthy marriage looks like, will help shape how they approach relationships in the future. Again, that doesn't mean we are not allowed mistakes but it does mean that we have an opportunity to model for these children what a marriage should look like in terms of how they should expect to be treated, and how they should expect to treat another. It's also an opportunity to show them what it looks like to serve God as a couple.

Finally, we must also remember that our individual walk with God continues even after we marry. God continues to have an individual purpose for each of us even when we are sharing our life with someone else, so we want to be our best not only for our spouse but also for God. For those who hunger to be used by Him, we must realize the more we grow in maturity, (emotionally and spiritually), the greater capacity we have to be used by Him in powerful ways. Even Jesus, the Son of God, the Beginning and the End, went through a growing process as we're told in Luke 2:52: *"and Jesus grew in wisdom and stature, and in favor with God and man."* If Jesus needed to grow to fulfill His purpose, we certainly need to do the same. God's Kingdom is a living, moving thing. It is not staying in one place, killing time until Jesus comes back. If we want to be part of that Kingdom, we cannot be stagnate. We have to be moving and growing as the Kingdom does.

Questions for Thought or Discussion

1. Why do you think it's important that we give our best to God and others?

2. How do you define what your "best" is? What specifically does that look like to you?

3. Be honest with yourself. How prepared do you feel for the "test" of marriage? What do you think you need to do to begin investing in that relationship even before it happens?

~ Six ~
Get Your House in Order

We've seen how dealing with our own issues is crucial in choosing God's best for us. It's also crucial in becoming God's best for someone else. In chapter 2 we talked about the parable of the seed sower (Matthew 13). What is the condition of your heart? Are you like the hard ground, unwilling to accept God's leading so there is never new growth in your life? Are you humble enough to recognize the areas in which you need to grow? Sitting here, reading this now, can you name the thing or things that are issues for you that you need to deal with, or have you convinced yourself that *you're* fine, it's everyone *else* who has the problem? Refusing to look at our own emotional wounds is like changing lanes in traffic without looking in the side and rear-view mirrors. Because you chose not to look for the car in the other lane doesn't mean it's not there, nor does it mean there won't be serious consequences if you chose to change lanes without looking first.

Most families grow up with at least one or two unwritten rules. These are things that are understood to be true, but no one ever actually talks about. For some of you, the unwritten rule in your family may have been, "If we don't talk about it, it's not real." Your family may have been good about walking around the proverbial elephant in the living room, never talking about the fact that it was there. And you may have even almost been able to convince yourself that it wasn't really there, or at least if it was, it wasn't a problem. But elephants in the living room are always a problem. Maybe the elephant in your family was addiction, or abuse, or poverty, or mental illness. Maybe the elephant in your own life right now is one of those things to ignore, but keeps gnawing away at your heart. Maybe it's an insecurity you just keep trying to ignore but keeps gnawing away at your heart. Whatever it is, I encourage you to name it and ask God to help you begin to deal with it.

Whenever we hold on to emotional wounds, it leaves the door open for Satan to operate in our lives. He will use whatever our weaknesses are to try and steal our joy and peace. What better time to work on ourselves than during this season of singleness? Once we're married, there are even more distractions around to keep us from getting our healing. Perhaps God has given us this time to grow so that we can be prepared for what He has to come. Let's not shy away from getting our emotional and spiritual house in order. The fewer emotional wounds we carry into a marriage, the healthier that relationship will be.

Getting our house in order is about preparing ourselves. God knows what the future holds for us and what we need to be equipped with to deal with it. Sometimes singles (myself included) fantasize about how wonderful it will be when we're married, forgetting that sometimes couples go through some incredible trials. We may have to deal with the loss of a child, death of a spouse at a young age, cancer or other debilitating illness, financial strain, etc. Are you strong enough, sitting here today, to be able to handle those things? Do you know how to plug into God's strength to get you through? If you can't do it now, you will not be able to do it any better because you're married.

I also want to be clear that we are all responsible for getting our own houses in order. Just as it is not our responsibility to fix anyone else, it is not anyone else's obligation to fix us. Our spouse can love us, pray with us, and encourage us, but they cannot do the emotional and spiritual work *for* us. If you're insecure about yourself now, getting married will not fix that for you; in fact, those insecurities may ultimately cause more problems in the relationship. Insecurities affect how we perceive others look at us and how we relate to them. They can cause us to become self-centered, manipulative, needy, withdrawn or self-sabotaging, sometimes without us even realizing it. If you are waiting to deal with painful issues because you think it will be easier when you have someone to go through it with you, *don't*. Deal with it now. Take owner-ship and decide that now is the time to improve. Again, the less baggage we take with us into a marriage, the happier and healthier that relationship will be.

In part one, we looked at using the fruits of the Spirit to gauge where someone else is at spiritually. Now, let's hold ourselves up to that gauge. To review, the fruits of the Spirit are love, joy, peace, patience, kindness, good-ness, faithfulness, gentleness and self-control (Galatians 5:22). If we are honest with ourselves, can we see evidence of these in our lives? All these fruits are important tools for us to have to be healthy in any relationship. If we have not allowed the Spirit to develop faithfulness and self-control in us, how will we resist temptation when it comes along? Many couples, (especially in marriage counseling), lack gentleness, kindness and patience in relating to each other, and so they fight often, in ways that are hurtful and de-structive to the relationship. Without allowing the Spirit to change us and grow these fruits in us, any marriage is going to be a serious challenge, and not likely to be happy or healthy.

Getting our house in order also requires us to know ourselves. As I mentioned earlier, just as each couple has a destiny and a purpose, so do we as individuals, and this does not stop because we get married. In Jeremiah 29:11, God assures us that He knows the plans He has for us. It is so important that we, while we are single, invest in our relationship with God so that we are firmly established in our walk with Him and have our own individual identity in Him *before* we get married. Being married is about *sharing* your walk with God, not sitting on your behind while your spouse does all the spiritual work. We don't get to ride on someone else's coattails. We are all accountable to God for our own spiritual growth.

Just as it's important to be able to hear and recognize the Spirit's voice in choosing a spouse, it will continue to be important in marriage. Life is filled with decisions that can sometimes significantly alter the course of our life. While seeking wise counsel can be invaluable when we're faced with these types of decisions, we are the ones that ultimately must decide. It's *so* important that we know how to hear from God in our own right, and not be dependent on someone else (spouse, pastor, etc.) to tell us what God is saying to us. Yes, they can help us get clarity or perspective and offer some direction, but we as individuals still have to take that back to God in prayer before moving forward. That's part of what it means to be in a relationship with Him! We talk with Him and listen to His voice as He speaks to us. I once heard a pastor say depression comes when we take our eyes off God's promises and focus on our circumstances. God is bigger than our circumstances! He causes all things to work together for the good of those who love Him (Romans 8:28). Learning to focus on God, His promises and His truth rather than looking to our circumstances or other people to tell us what's going to happen and help us get through hard times without falling into despair. If we can get into that habit now, it will surely serve us well in marriage. In order to succeed, however, we must first know how to recognize His voice on our own.

Questions for Thought or Discussion

1. What are some emotional wounds you can identify in yourself? In what ways do you think it is important for you to begin to deal with those areas? How might they negatively affect your relationships?

2. How do you see the fruits of the Spirit manifesting in your life? What fruits do you see a lot of, and what fruits would you like to see more of?

3. What things do you do now to tap into God's strength when you are dealing with trials? How might this be helpful for you in marriage?

4. How strong do you feel about your relationship with God as it is now? In what areas to you feel you may need to grow or strengthen your relationship with Him to better prepare you for marriage?

~ Seven ~
Relating To Others

Equally important to looking inward, is looking outward at how we relate to others now. If we struggle in relationships now, we are likely to struggle in marriage because we will repeat the mistakes we are making now. We need to look at our relationships with family, friends and coworkers to see patterns of relating to other people that could potentially cause problems in a marriage. For example, what kind of a friend are we? If we struggle to be loyal, supportive, giving, thoughtful, encouraging and kind to our friends, we will not be able to be those things for a spouse.

Maybe you are someone who feels like you don't really like people. Maybe you tend to have a temper and blow up at people, or perhaps you are distant and isolative. Whatever the root of the issue, it may be related to a wounded area of your heart that needs healing. Maybe you carry around anger over some past hurt that has become like an infected sore, and as it festers, it affects how you interact with other people.

I spent several years being so angry with God because I was still single, that I pulled away from Him. I decided, "From now on, You and I are in a business relationship and that's it. You're the boss, and I'm Your employee, but that's where it ends, because this is *not* what I signed up for." I stopped listening to worship music, and even stopped praying. Oh, I went to church, but I was only going through the motions, as if I were attending a staff meeting. In that time, my heart became so resentful and bitter that I became a moody, irritable, cranky person that could not have been enjoyable for others to be around, and it was someone I didn't want to be. I was so focused on my own pain that I know I missed many oppor-

tunities to reach out to other people, as well as oppor-
tunities to enjoy every precious moment I am given in this
world. I eventually realized I could not keep going through
life being miserable because I refused to accept that things
hadn't turned out the way I expected. I began to plug into
God and ask Him to help me trust that He was leading me
through this singleness for a reason, and learn to enjoy my
life while I have it. It took some time but because I asked
Him to change my heart, He did.

 For some, the issue isn't anger towards others, but
rather, a lack of trust in others. Somewhere along the line,
you got hurt and decided life was a lot safer behind a thick
wall that keeps other people out, and your heart safe. If
you're naturally an introverted per-son to start with, you
probably already struggle to get outside yourself, add a
broken heart to that mix, and it's easy to retreat completely behind that wall and not let others in. The ironic
thing about walls is, while they serve their purpose in
protecting us, they can also isolate us from experiencing
genuine, deep connections with other people, and that is a
lonely place. Even if you'll never be a social butterfly, you
still need people in your life. We all do. We're programmed
that way. The danger in living an isolated life is that we
build a fantasy in our mind and believe if we could meet
that one special person, we can let them in, open our heart
to only them and never be lonely again. That person will fix
the problem, make our loneliness go away and we won't
have to step outside our comfort zone in the process.

 The problem with this fantasy is just that—it's a
fantasy. The reality is, if we aren't letting people in now,
we will never allow ourselves to trust someone enough to
let them share our life and heart. A marriage requires a
deep level of trust and emotional intimacy. If you're a
hermit now, living behind well-fortified emotional walls,
how in the world will you be able to share the level of intimacy and trust a marriage needs? The moment that person

disappoints you, the wall will go back up and you'll have distance in your marriage—and marriage can be a lonely place if you're not connecting with your spouse. It's important to recognize that a person living an isolated life is a person living in *fear*.

Yes, it's extremely important to have healthy boundaries, and exercise caution until we know another person is safe and healthy for us. However, that is not the same as letting fear rule our choices. As 2 Timothy 1:7 says, *"For the Spirit God gave us does not make us timid, but gives us power, love and self-discipline."* Stepping out in faith and taking a risk may cause anxiety. But when we trust God, His Holy Spirit will bring us peace in the midst of our anxiety. Fear keeps us isolated from others, and stops us from taking steps God is asking we take in order to lead us to *the one* He has for us. By contrast, the Holy Spirit will give us strength and peace to press forward de-spite any uncomfortable feelings we have. As David de-scribes in Psalm 27:1, *"The Lord is my light and my sal-vation—whom shall I fear? The Lord is the stronghold of my life—of whom shall I be afraid?"*

Whether it's anger or fear, when there are barriers in our relationships, we need to acknowledge that we may have people we need to forgive. Not forgiving someone gives Satan a foothold to move us into bitterness, which is as toxic as any fast-spreading cancer. It taints our perception of ourselves and others, and frankly, it keeps us stuck —exactly where Satan wants us. Think about it, if God's plan is to use you and your spouse to impact this world for Him, and further His Kingdom, does Satan want that to happen? No. He will do anything to keep you from fulfilling your destiny.

The issue of forgiveness could be a separate book entirely, so for this book, let us focus on the fact that holding a grudge is yet another type of "baggage" we do not want to carry into a marriage. In fact, it's possible, if we don't deal with it, we may never get to the marriage God has for us because of the negative way it causes us to relate to others.

If you're struggling in your connections with people, I encourage you to ask God to give you His heart for human-kind. Just like our spouses should have God's heart for us, we should have His heart for our spouse. What better way to grow in that area than by seeking God's heart for people in our life right now? You might even ask Him to give you His heart about your current situation. This is something we are going to need to be able to do when we're married—ask God for His heart about our marriage, our circumstances and trials, and where our life together is headed.

Maybe, if you're honest with yourself, you know you tend to be judgmental. Ask God to help soften your heart in this area. Being judgmental is something that can do such damage to an otherwise loving relationship. Instead, ask God to help you see others with more compassion. It will help increase your patience with others, and anyone who's been married will tell you no matter how much you love someone, marriage requires a lot of patience. If you're afraid to trust, ask God to help you break free of fear, use wisdom, and be able to see the good in people. Have you been wronged and can't get over it? Ask God to help you forgive so you can be free of resentment and embrace the future He has for you.

When we revisit Corinthians 13, we see how God tells us we should love people—with patience, kindness, keeping no record of wrongs, not dishonoring them, not being self-seeking, not envying them, rejoicing in the truth, not proud or boasting, and not easily angered. The more we become like Christ, the more we will be able to love in these ways.

In my past experience with counseling married couples, I saw so many husbands and wives struggling be-cause they entered into disagreements with the intent to win and prove they were right, rather than work it out in a way that honors the other person. In the heat of the moment name calling began, followed by throwing in old, sore subjects to add fuel to the fire— "You know, you're being a real jerk. This is like the time you did _____. You were wrong then and you're wrong now!"

Instead of working toward a solution, they hurt each other, and the chasm between them grew wider. Love is more than a feeling of affection and attraction to someone else, it is an *action*. It is expressed in the sum of our words *and* behaviors toward others. These words and behaviors can hurt, or they can heal. They can build up, or they can tear down. They can bring encouragement, or they can bring destruction.

Communication is another topic that could be a whole separate book in itself, so for now I will say that learning how to communicate effectively, (verbally or non-verbally), in a way that is loving and honors your commitment to each other, is incredibly important and something we can be developing now as singles to equip us for marriage. Individual counseling, self-help books and workshops, can be helpful in this area. Also, if you become engaged to be married, make sure your pastor or counselor covers communication as part of premarital counseling.

Another important area of our heart we need to check is our level of selfishness in relationships. Ever encounter one of those people who talks your ear off, never once asking, "Oh, by the way, how are you?" It's amazing how much we like to talk about *us*, think about *us*, and make sure we get what we think we have coming to *us*.

However, if we enter relationships focused on "self" and putting "self" first, it will damage the relationship. Selfishness is part of what is behind name-calling and saying hurtful things, because that person is more concerned about winning the fight, than in preserving the relationship. It damages trust because selfish people are

not usually selfish only occasionally. It's typically an ac-
cumulation of things that happen every day—making sure
they feed themselves at dinner first, not attending events
that are important to the other person because they have
their own interests to pursue, being wasteful, and chronic-
ally interrupting because they have a bigger and better
story to tell than you, are just a few examples. Every time
that person chooses to be selfish, it sends the message, "I
don't care about you, I only care about me." In short, it's
hurtful. Rather than pro-mote growth in the relationship, it
causes division.

Now, I want to be clear. We are not called to be
doormats, or martyrs, who never think about our self, and
only think of other people. Balance is important for our
well-being. We are no good to anyone if we don't take care
of ourselves. In part one, we talked about the importance
of having healthy boundaries when choosing a spouse.
Healthy boundaries are also important in order for us to be
God's best for someone else. Never taking care of ourselves
sends the message to others that, "I don't care about myself, and you don't need to either." Keep in mind, sometimes our spouses will need us to hold them accountable so
they can grow. Sometimes, we have to be mirrors for each
other, even in friendships. That means saying *no* at times,
setting limits, and being assertive enough to lovingly confront people when needed. There have been times in my
life, if someone had not loved me enough to say, "Hey, you
need to work on this!" I might never have found the cour-
age to do so.

Simply put, one of the most important ways we can
assure we are God's best for someone else, is to dedicate
ourselves to becoming more like Jesus. The more God
changes our heart to be like His, the more our behavior
lines up with His heart, and we become more loving,
patient, merciful and gracious people, characteristics that
help a marriage flourish.

Questions for Thought or Discussion

1. What do you think your friends would say about the kind of friend you are to them? In what ways do you think you could be a better friend to people?

2. Do you see evidence of selfishness in your relationships now? How so? How does it affect those relationships? What might you do to begin to change that?

3. To what degree have you been a doormat in your relationships? How did it affect you? How have you learned to not repeat that role, or what might you do to help you change that pattern?

4. How well have you loved others the way 1 Corinthians defines love? What parts of that scripture do you think you do well, and what parts do you think you need to work on?

5. How do you handle conflict in relationships? In what ways do you think you've learned to handle disagreements effectively, and in what ways do you still struggle?

In Summary

My hope is, if you only walk away with one thing from this book, it is that marriage is meant to be so much more than romance and great sex. It is meant to be a relationship in which two people love God even more than they love each other, and want to serve Him, and have their marriage used by Him, to make a difference in His Kingdom.

It is meant to be a relationship in which two people grow and flourish. It is meant to be a source of joy. In order to have that kind of marriage, however, we must prepare. We must examine ourselves, look at how we choose a mate, and ask God to show us the areas we need to grow in to be ready for marriage. Because of the spiritual significance of marriage, it is crucial that we, "*Seek first His Kingdom and His righteousness, and all these things will be given to you.*" (Matthew 6:33).

God is always pursuing us with such passion! If we pursue Him, He will change our hearts and minds to be like His, so that we can choose and be His best in all areas of our lives.

~ End ~

If you would like to contact the author, please use the following e-mail:

jenifer@ourfaithapplied.com

Statistics from the Center for Disease Control are taken from:
http://www.cdc.gov/nchs/data/nvsr/nvsr58/nvsr58_25.pdf
Statistics from the U.S. Census Bureau are taken from:
http://www.census.gov/prod/cen2010/briefs/c2010br-14.pdf

www.ingramcontent.com/pod-product-compliance
Lightning Source LLC
Chambersburg PA
CBHW060539030426
42337CB00021B/4347